GREAT FILMMAKERS
SOFIA COPPOLA

Susan Dudley Gold

Cavendish
Square

New York

For Melodie Provost, valued friend, best walking buddy, and amazing Project Linus coordinator

Published in 2015 by Cavendish Square Publishing, LLC,
243 5th Avenue, Suite 136, New York, NY 10016

First Edition

Website: cavendishsq.com

This publication represents the opinions and views of the author based on his or her personal experience, knowledge, and research. The information in this book serves as a general guide only. The author and publisher have used their best efforts in preparing this book and disclaim liability rising directly or indirectly from the use and application of this book.

CPSIA Compliance Information: Batch #WS14CSQ

All websites were available and accurate when this book was sent to press.

Library of Congress Cataloging-in-Publication Data

Gold, Susan Dudley.
Sofia Coppola / by Susan Dudley Gold.
p. cm. — (Great filmmakers)
Includes index.
ISBN 978-1-62712-945-9 (hardcover) ISBN 978-1-62712-947-3 (ebook)
1. Coppola, Sofia, 1971- — Juvenile literature. 2. Motion picture producers and directors — United States — Biography — Juvenile literature. 3. Women motion picture producers and directors — United States — Biography — Juvenile literature. I. Gold, Susan Dudley. II. Title.
PN1998.3.C672 G86 2015
791.43—d23

Editorial Director: Dean Miller	Senior Designer: Amy Greenan
Senior Editor: Fletcher Doyle	Production Manager: Jennifer Ryder-Talbot
Senior Copy Editor: Wendy A. Reynolds	Production Editor: David McNamara
Art Director: Jeffrey Talbot	Photo Researcher: J8 Media

The photographs in this book are used by permission and through the courtesy of: Cover and page 1, Jun Sato/WireImage/Getty Images; AP Photo/Randy Rasmussen, 5; AFP/Getty Images, 6; Vince Bucci/Getty Images, 9; David McGough/The LIFE Picture Collection/Time & Life Pictures/Getty Images, 10; Ron Galella Collection/WireImage/Getty Images, 11; pagadesign/E+/Getty Images, 12, 24, 38, 50, 58, 64; www.demilked.com/free-paper-textures-backgrounds, 12–13, 24–25, 38–39, 50–51, 58, 64; Jamie McCarthy/Getty Images, 13; © Photos 12/Alamy, 14; © Paramount Pictures/Entertainment Pictures/ZUMAPRESS.com, 15; Chris Weeks/Hulton Archive/Getty Images, 19; Frank Micelotta/Getty Images, 21; MARTIN BUREAU/AFP/Getty Images, 25; ZOETROPE STUDIOS/Album/Newscom, 26; Matthew Eisman/Getty Images, 29; Randall Michelson Archive/WireImage/Getty Images, 30–31; Lawrence Lucier/Getty Images, 33; © FOCUS FEATURES/ZUMAPRESS.com, 36; Fotos International/Getty Images, 39; Frederick M. Brown/Getty Images, 41; © Columbia Pictures/Entertainment Pictures, ZUMAPRESS.com, 45; Raphael GAILLARDE/Gamma-Rapho/Getty Images, 48; Kevin Winter/Getty Images, 51; Bertrand Rindoff Petroff/French Select/Getty Images, 53; Bryan Bedder/Getty Images, 55; Kiyoshi Ota/Getty Images, 56; ALBERTO PIZZOLI/AFP/Getty Images, 60; Ian Gavan/Getty Images, 63; Jason Kempin/Getty Images, 64; AFP/Getty Images, 66.

Printed in the United States of America

GREAT FILMMAKERS
SOFIA COPPOLA

1 EARLY YEARS

Sofia Coppola got her first break in Hollywood in 1971 when she was only a few weeks old. She played the role of Michael Francis Rizzi, the baby boy christened in *The Godfather*. The epic movie won her father, Francis Ford Coppola, Golden Globe awards for best motion picture and best director, and an Academy Award for best screenwriting. He also was nominated for an Oscar for best director.

Sofia Coppola, however, received no mention in the movie's credits.

Fast-forward thirty-three years, and Sofia Coppola received plenty of attention for her film *Lost in Translation*. She wrote and directed the movie, a romantic comedy-drama starring Bill Murray and Scarlett Johansson. Coppola collected Academy Award nominations for best director and best original screenplay. It was the first time an American woman had ever been nominated for a best director Oscar. Peter Jackson won the

4

Ten-year-old Sofia with her parents, filmmakers Francis Ford Coppola and Eleanor Coppola.

Sofia Coppola received the Oscar for best original screenplay in 2004 for *Lost In Translation*.

best director award that year for *Lord of the Rings: Return of the King*, but Coppola won an Oscar for her screenplay, the story about an alliance formed between an aging movie star and the lonely, recently married young woman he meets in Tokyo.

The film also earned Coppola a Golden Globe for best screenplay. In addition, she received the Lina Mangiacapre Award at the Venice Film Festival, which is given to films that show "the changing image of women."

Scoring another milestone for women, Coppola in 2010 became the first American woman—and only the fourth American ever—to win the top prize at the Venice Festival. Her stark, contemplative film *Somewhere*, about a bad-boy actor whose eleven-year-old daughter's visit causes him to question his empty life, won the festival's Golden Lion. *The New York Times* applauded Coppola for creating "something marvelous," and said viewing *Somewhere* was "like reading a poem." Coppola has made the most impact writing and directing intimate stories that explore relationships between characters who are going through transitions in their lives.

With her connections to Hollywood through her famous father, she has been able to go places closed to many other young artists. In making her movies she convinced one of the most elegant hotels in the world, the Principe di Savoia in Milan, Italy, to allow her to film in its presidential suite. She talked her way into another prestigious hotel, Southern California's Chateau Marmont, where she and her crew and cast lived and filmed for two weeks. She also persuaded heiress Paris Hilton to allow filming inside her home to depict the real-life burglaries that occurred there.

Coppola often focuses on the lonely isolation of life on the inside in her movies. At the same time, she examines the longing of outsiders to get inside. Her trademark camera angles and point of view—a character gazing out a window or into the distance, a view of the world from over a character's shoulder, a close-up of a character's face and expressions with little or no dialogue—all serve to portray the character's isolation and loneliness and to draw the audience into the character's world. It is Coppola's genius that she can combine style and substance to create intelligent, complex characters in films that are both beautiful and deep.

Family Business

Making movies is the Coppola family business. Sofia's family tree is a Who's Who of famous actors, directors, and filmmakers. Her father had already won an Academy Award for best original screenplay for the film *Patton* and formed his own film company by the time she was born on May 12, 1971. Her mother, Eleanor Coppola, a designer and artist, makes documentary films. Her brother, Roman Coppola, serves as assistant director on many of her films. Her grandfather, Carmine Coppola, composed music and wrote movie scores. Her grandmother, Italia Coppola, was an actress. Her aunt, Talia Shire, costarred in the film *Rocky* and played the role of Connie Corleone in the three *Godfather* films. Her cousins, Nicolas Cage, Robert Schwartzman, and Jason Schwartzman, are all actors.

Sofia Carmina Coppola is the youngest child of Eleanor and Francis Ford Coppola. She and her brothers, Roman and Gian-Carlo, often accompanied their parents to faraway spots when their father filmed his movies. When Francis Ford Coppola filmed *The Godfather, Part II*, in 1974, Sofia, then three, watched the action seated in her own miniature director's chair with her name on it. When not on the road, the family lived in Napa Valley on a 1,700-acre estate. The property is also home to the family's vineyard, which produces wine under the Coppola name and Inglenook brand.

At age seven, Sofia Coppola spent her time drawing the palm trees of Manila during the filming

Nicolas Cage (Sofia Coppola's cousin), Francis Ford Coppola, Sofia Coppola, and Eleanor Coppola made the 2004 Golden Globe Awards after-party a family affair.

of *Apocalypse Now*, her father's powerful movie about the U.S. role in the Vietnam War. The family moved to Tulsa, Oklahoma, for the filming of *The Outsiders*, which was released in 1983. In it, Coppola made her feature film debut as an inquisitive young girl in a Dairy Queen parking lot.

A twelve-year-old Coppola had appeared before the cameras in another minor role in her father's next film, *Rumble Fish*. This time she played Donna, the younger sister of the lead's girlfriend. Sofia's cousin, Nicolas Cage, took on the character of Smokey, his first major role.

Her next film assignment came in 1984, when she played a child in the street in her father's gangster musical, *The Cotton Club*. That same year, she also appeared in *Frankenweenie*, a black-and-white, thirty-minute short directed by Tim Burton. The movie focuses on a young boy who brings his dog

Diane Lane, left, and Matt Dillon, right, stars of *Rumble Fish*, with Sofia Coppola in 1983 during the filming of the movie.

back to life using electricity. Wearing a blonde wig, Sofia played the role of Anne Chambers, a neighbor girl freaked out by the resurrected dog. The credits listed her as "Domino Coppola," a stage name she used at the time. It was the first film in which she appeared that was not directed by her father.

In the 1986 film *Peggy Sue Got Married*, directed by her father, Sofia was cast in a minor role as the estranged younger sister of the lead character, played by Kathleen Turner. She followed this with another minor role as Noodle in Polish film director Yurek Bogayevicz's 1987 film *Anna*.

Francis Ford Coppola included all of his children on the movie sets of the films he directed, put them to work acting and doing other tasks, and took them on location from one country to another as the movie required. As the only daughter, however, Sofia clearly holds a special place in the family.

Her relationship with her father is revealed in a number of ways. The family's winery, for example, offers Sofia sparkling wines in tribute to her. The company markets the wine "as bright and effervescent as the woman who inspired it," and notes that the line of wines "began as a gift from a father to his daughter."

Sofia remembers her father relaxing at home and cooking, playing opera full blast on the stereo, and entertaining a houseful of famous friends. "We did not have a boring childhood," Coppola confided to Lee Radziwill during a 2013 interview for the *New York Times*.

Family Tragedy

Tragedy struck the family in 1986, when Sofia was fifteen. Her twenty-two-year-old brother Gian-Carlo (called Gio by the family) died in a boating accident. He and a friend, Griffin Patrick O'Neal (the son of actor Ryan O'Neal), were boating on the South River

Francis Ford Coppola, center, with his two sons, Gio, left, and Roman, right, in 1986.

near Chesapeake Bay in Maryland on Memorial Day. Their motorboat, piloted by O'Neal, ran under the towline of another boat. Gian-Carlo suffered severe

FASHION ICON

When she was only fifteen, Sofia Coppola served a summer internship at the Chanel fashion house in Paris. In between pouring coffee and running errands, she watched head designer Karl Lagerfeld sketch his designs for fashion shows. Coppola would make many more forays into the world of fashion. In her twenties, she introduced her own line of clothing, a collection of about twenty designs featuring "baby Ts," nylon T-shirt dresses, pinstriped pants and skirts, and nylon nightie dresses. Coppola and her friend Stephanie Hayman launched the fashion line, called Milkfed, with a flashy photo shoot at the Chateau Marmont, where Zoe Cassavetes and other friends served as models. The venerable hotel, a Hollywood landmark, would later serve as the backdrop for her 2010 film *Somewhere*. Japanese buyers took over the line in later years and distribute the clothing in Japan today. Coppola also designs handbags for the exclusive French fashion house Louis Vuitton. In 2013, she designed windows for Le Bon Marché, a department store in Paris, which featured a miniature version of the Sofia bag.

In 2002, a topless Coppola coyly posed in an advertisement for a perfume by fashion designer Marc Jacobs (with Coppola below). She has done modeling jobs for Jacobs, *Vogue* magazine, and others. The phrase "simple yet elegant" has often been used to describe her style, her looks, and her persona. It is part of what has made her a fashion icon.

Coppola has lent her directorial skill to those in the fashion world as well. Among her fashion film projects are advertising videos for Miss Dior Chérie perfume and the 2012 Marni collection designed by Consuelo Castiglioni. In 2013, the Marc Jacobs fashion house hired her to direct a twenty-one second commercial to advertise its Daisy perfume.

Francis and Sofia Coppola on the set of *New York Stories* in 1989. They co-wrote a segment of the film.

head injuries when he was thrown onto the deck. He was dead by the time rescue workers delivered him to a nearby hospital. The *New York Times* reported that O'Neal escaped with a minor injury to his shoulder. O'Neal later pleaded guilty to negligent operation of a boat after Maryland prosecuted him for manslaughter.

When the call came about the accident, Francis Coppola was filming the movie *Gardens of Stone* in Washington, D.C. He called his wife and daughter with the terrible news. "Gio was that kind of enchanting older brother who would take me on adventures and treat me like an adult," Sofia told the *New York Times* years later. His death, she said, was heartbreaking. "You never really get over something like that."

Sofia went into therapy to deal with her grief. She healed, she said, but "it becomes a part of who you are."

Two years later, in 1988, seventeen-year-old Coppola shared writing duties with her father on a segment of a quirky film about life in New York

City. *New York Stories* consisted of three parts, each
directed by a big-name director. Francis Ford Coppola's
segment, "Life Without Zoe," was about a twelve-
year-old girl living in a grand hotel while her parents
tour the world. The experience became a tutorial in
directing and screenwriting for the young Sofia.

Critics did not respond well to the father-daughter
effort. "Life Without Zoe," critic Roger Ebert said,
lacked purpose. "Nothing holds together on an
emotional or plot level," Ebert wrote. Despite the
disappointing reception, the experience gave Sofia
valuable lessons in how to develop an idea into a
script, and then mold the script into a film.

Sofia as Mary
Corleone in
*The Godfather
Part III*, with
Andy Garcia.

Sofia as Mary Corleone

Coppola's next major step in film came a year
later when she was eighteen. A freshman at Mills
College in Oakland, California, studying art history,
Sofia had flown to Rome to celebrate Christmas
with her family. The Coppolas were in Italy to film
The Godfather Part III, the third and final story of

the Corleone family. Francis Coppola presented his daughter with a tantalizing opportunity. He asked her to play the role of Mary Corleone, daughter of the lead character, Michael Corleone. Winona Ryder had been slated to fill the role, but had withdrawn because of exhaustion. Sofia Coppola agreed to take on the part. She took time off from school and began filming almost immediately. It seemed like a good career move to her at the time. She told an interviewer for *The Guardian* years later that she had been exploring different things and figured she should give acting a try. "I was game," she said.

Sofia had had minor roles in several of her father's films, but she lacked the training and experience required of an actor in a role as demanding as that of Mary Corleone. Few people supported the choice of Sofia for the role. The fact that Coppola would cast his untrained daughter in such a major role did not sit well with either the producers or some of the film's established actors. They expressed shock when Coppola brought Sofia on the set and explained her role in the movie. Even her aunt, Talia Shire, who played Michael Corleone's sister in the movie, said she feared that her niece might not be ready for the role.

For Sofia, the role was challenging and the pressure was daunting. She tried her best to meet the demands of the job. "My whole life I've had to prove myself," she told *Entertainment Weekly* after the film was released. "Catching up on years of acting training was the most difficult."

Eleanor Coppola wrote in her diary about her daughter's struggles during the filming. In January 1990 she wrote that Sofia had to follow a hectic schedule of going to costume fittings, having her hair done, and performing for the cameras.

Her daughter also studied with a diction teacher in an attempt to sound more like the Italian American daughter of a crime boss instead of a Valley Girl from California. "Several times," her mother wrote, "she has burst into tears."

A torrent of criticism greeted the film's release in 1990, much of it directed at Sofia's portrayal of Mary Corleone. Film critic Bryan Walsh wrote mockingly of her "attempting to emote." Almost all of the reviewers noted that the third *Godfather* movie did not measure up to the previous two. Its "ludicrous plot twists" and "half-baked" script kept it from being a masterpiece. Nevertheless, many critics praised the movie's overall accomplishments.

The film won a "thumbs-up" from Gene Siskel and his co-critic Ebert and earned high marks for being, as the *Baltimore Sun* put it, "painfully genuine." Other reviewers called it a "rich, resonant and deeply felt conclusion" to the *Godfather* saga, and "the work of a masterful filmmaker."

There were few kind words for Sofia Coppola, however. She won two **Golden Raspberry (Razzie) Awards**, given for bad performances, for worst supporting actress and worst new star. Longtime fans of the previous *Godfather* movies bitterly harped at Coppola's choice of his daughter to portray Mary. At the press screening of the film in December 1990, audience members actually laughed at her death scene.

Coppola herself was less devastated by the bad reviews than other aspiring actors might have been. She said she never really wanted to be an actress. Even so, she acknowledged to *New York Times* film critic Graham Fuller that the critical response "was definitely painful." She said she uses the experience to help her relate to the actors she directs.

2 IN THE DIRECTOR'S CHAIR

After the *Godfather* debacle, Coppola took a break from film. She turned her sights instead to the art world. She returned to school, taking art courses at the California Institute of the Arts (CalArts). "I wanted to be a painter," she told reporter Carrie Rickey in 2013. "They told me I wasn't."

She had better luck at photography, which she studied at the Art Center College of Design. The instructor praised her use of point of view in her work. She carried that knowledge with her when she resumed her interest in film. However, most of what she learned about filmmaking, she said, came from her father. "We were always talking about and looking at film," she told Rickey. "I didn't even realize I was learning."

Coppola dabbled in many careers in the 1990s. Her interest in fashion and style led to a job designing costumes for *The Spirit of '76*, a spoof of 1970s life in America. She also did an uncredited cameo as a girl in the parade in the film. The movie,

Sofia Coppola, seen here at the Costume Designers Guild Awards in Beverly Hills, California, in 2001, has become a fashion icon with her sleek style and elegant sense of design.

cowritten and produced by her brother Roman, was filmed in California.

After leaving school, she and her friend Zoe Cassavetes created *Hi Octane*, a TV variety show for the Comedy Central network. The women co-hosted the series, which premiered in 1994. It featured performances of several music groups, including the Beastie Boys and Flea from the Red Hot Chili Peppers. Photographer Andrew Durham directed the show, which lasted only four episodes.

Coppola held a series of jobs in the fashion and music business. She modeled for Banana Republic and DKNY ads, performed in music videos for Madonna and rock bands Sonic Youth and the Black Crowes, and worked as a contributing editor for *Details*, a men's fashion magazine.

During this time, Coppola worked with her brother Roman on several of his music videos. While on the set for the filming of a music video for Sonic Youth in 1992, she met Spike Jonze, the young director of the project. The two would later marry. The video eventually led to a contract as a cameraman for Jonze and later as a director for Satellite Films. In 1993, Coppola and Jonze collaborated on a music video for the song "Shine" by Walt Mink, an indie rock band. Jonze edited the video, which Coppola produced. Its dreamlike images depicted the same type of bored, rich, beautiful people who would later populate her films.

In 1996, Coppola codirected *Bed, Bath and Beyond* with her friend, actress Ione Skye, and Andrew Durham. The twenty-eight-minute comedy tells the story of a French director, his shapely wife, who wants the title role in her husband's latest film, and his Latin mistress. Jonze and Coppola's brother Roman shared cinematography duties on the film.

The Coppola family, from left, Sofia, Francis, Eleanor, and Roman, gathered at the Cannes Film Festival in France in 2001.

Debut as a Director

Coppola's debut as a solo director came with the release in 1998 of *Lick the Star*, a stylish, fourteen-minute black-and-white short produced on sixteen millimeter film. She and Stephanie Hayman cowrote the film, which examines death from a teenager's viewpoint. Coppola would revisit that topic in her first feature film, *The Virgin Suicides*.

Lick the Star opens with a close-up shot of a young teen, Kate, peering out of the window of the car delivering her to seventh grade. She is confined to crutches, after her father ran over her toe with his car. Kate joins her friends in the "select" gang of girls, headed by Chlöe, a sultry seventh grader. The girls, who bully anyone whose path crosses theirs, become obsessed by the novel *Flowers in the Attic*, in which a mother poisons her children with arsenic to inherit the family wealth. The girls plan to slowly poison the boys they dislike and obtain rat poison for the job. Before the plan can be carried out, Chlöe makes an offhand remark that is misinterpreted as racist. After the whole school turns against her, she tries to commit suicide by overdosing on aspirin and drowning in a tub amid floating roses. The attempt fails, and she finds herself alone when she returns to school, the butt of rude remarks that she once hurled.

Coppola's short contains many of the elements that she would use in her later work. Its dreamy mood, focus on characters trapped in their own world, and many distinct stylistic touches would all be repeated in her subsequent films. The story is told with a distinctive voice that is Coppola's alone: the opening scene of a character looking wistfully out of a car window, close-ups of faces that quickly cut away to other scenes, the use of rock music. In this first film, as in her later movies, Coppola tapped her friends and acquaintances to fill roles as cast and crew. The actor and director Peter Bogdanovich played a cameo role as the principal. Sofia's friend Zoe Cassavetes, a screenwriter, actress, and director, also appeared briefly in the film. Famed cinematographer Lance Acord provided the elegant black-and-white photography. Pam Cook, a leading film expert and professor of film, has called *Lick the Star* "a stylish, confident achievement that paved the way for Coppola's first feature, *The Virgin Suicides*."

Despite the critics' treatment of her after *Godfather III*, Coppola had not totally given up on acting. For fun, she played a cameo role as the handmaiden Saché in director George Lucas'

Star Wars Episode I: The Phantom Menace in 1999. Coppola knew Lucas, who lived near her family home in California. Her efforts earned her another nomination—but no win—for a Razzie Award, this time as worst supporting actress. Fortunately, she escaped the brutal flogging she endured for her portrayal of Mary Corleone.

By then, Coppola had become absorbed in *The Virgin Suicides*, a haunting tale of five beautiful teenage sisters who commit suicide. The book, written by Jeffrey Eugenides, captured Coppola's imagination. "I loved the book," she said at the Sundance Film Festival in 2000. It was both funny and tragic, a book that she soon realized would make a wonderful movie. Drawn to the book's dark depiction of adolescent sexuality, she began writing a script based on the 1993 novel. Muse Productions, which owned the rights to the book, had started its own screenplay. When they read Coppola's version, however, company executives liked hers better and decided to give her a chance. "I felt so strongly about *The Virgin Suicides* that I never stopped to think about the end result or that people would actually watch it," she later told the *New York Times*.

First Feature Film

In 1998, Coppola, then twenty-seven, directed *The Virgin Suicides*, her first feature film. She said her brother Gio's death probably influenced her handling of the script and the subsequent filming. "I think some of that sadness went into *The Virgin Suicides*," she told Lynn Hirschberg of the *New York Times*. "I think I'm always drawn to projects that help me understand something about myself."

SOFIA COPPOLA'S MUSIC

Music plays a key role—even with its absence—in all of Sofia Coppola's films. She is meticulous in getting just the right sound to amplify each scene. The tunes in her first feature film, *The Virgin Suicides*, are the songs of teens who grew up in the mid-1970s. Works by the Hollies, Carole King, Al Green, the Bee Gees, and Styx help the boys and girls communicate as they swap songs over the telephone and dance to the beat. Music from other eras—Sloan's songs from the 1990s and a score composed by the French band Air—lend a dreamlike quality to the movie. Thomas Mars, who would later become Coppola's second husband, sang the movie's theme song, "Playground Love" by Air.

Lost in Translation, about two lonely people who meet at a hotel in Tokyo, demanded music that, in Coppola's words, would evoke "a sense of disassociation, of being in this kind of unfamiliar, alienating world." To achieve the sound, Coppola and her music guru Brian Reitzell turned to Kevin Shields, the lead singer

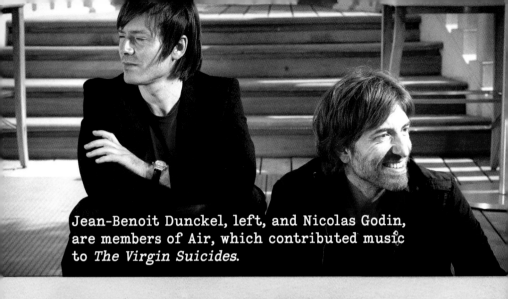

Jean-Benoit Dunckel, left, and Nicolas Godin, are members of Air, which contributed music to *The Virgin Suicides*.

of the Irish alternative rock band My Bloody Valentine. Shields contributed one of the band's songs and created new music for the movie.

Coppola switched to post-punk rock for *Marie Antoinette*. Some viewers objected to Coppola's use of pop music as totally inappropriate for a movie set in the eighteenth century. But others agreed with the director that the vibrant tunes conveyed Marie's youthful vigor and helped modern viewers relate to the teenage queen.

The scarcity of music in *Somewhere* emphasizes the lead character's isolation and the almost total emptiness of his life. Music does play an important role in the film, however. The score, by Phoenix, which includes the band's "Love Like a Sunset," creates a moody, subtle backdrop as the film unfolds.

For the blatant, out-there action of *The Bling Ring*, Coppola relied on Kanye West's hip-hop, and pop rap pieces like Rick Ross's "9 Piece" and Reema Major's "Gucci Bag" echoed the message as well as the mood of the scenes.

Leslie Hayman, Kirsten Dunst, A. J. Cook, and Chelse Swain played sisters in *The Virgin Suicides*.

The movie takes place in the 1970s in an upscale suburb of Detroit, Michigan. The opening credits play against a lush panorama of all the paraphernalia of young teen girlhood: luminous pink pearls, a blue-handled mascara stick, a cream-colored jewelry box, and a coral heart-shaped barrette. We see a girl lying on a bed reading, applying makeup and putting on earrings, taking a record off a phonograph, walking barefoot on a carpet around clothes scattered across the room, drawing hearts in a diary. From this normal American girl's bedroom, the camera seamlessly travels to the shocking image of the feet and legs of a girl who has clearly hung herself, her feet clad in sensible tan shoes with laces neatly tied. Edward Lachman, who directed the film's

26

photography, captures the scenes in a gauzy haze, as through the fuzzy lens of memory.

The story is told from the point of view of four adolescent boys who are obsessed with the five beautiful Lisbon sisters. The movie is narrated by a now-middle-aged man (Giovanni Ribisi), who speaks for the boys, as he recounts the tragic story of the mysterious Lisbon girls from his youth. The action begins with the suicide attempt of the youngest sister, thirteen-year-old Cecilia, who has slit her wrists in the bathtub. An ambulance carries her to the hospital, where she recovers enough to go home. On the advice of a counselor, the Lisbons decide to hold a party to cheer Cecilia. While the others are drinking punch and listening to music in the family room, Cecilia commits suicide by jumping out of her bedroom window. The rest of the sisters—Lux, Bonnie, Therese, and Mary—will follow suit by the end of the movie. The boys pore through Cecilia's diary and a photo album of the family in their efforts to make sense of the events leading up to the girls' suicides. Coppola shot the movie in full frame, she said, because the format looked more like photos in a scrapbook.

The community, shocked by Cecilia's death, delivers flowers to the grieving family. Workers dig up the iron fence where Cecilia impaled herself. As summer passes into fall, the remaining sisters return to school. Their father, a math teacher at the high school the sisters attend, buries himself in his work. None of the girls are allowed to date.

The school's bad boy, Trip, seduces Lux, the most adventurous of the sisters, and convinces her father to let him take her to the prom. The parents agree, but only on the condition that all four surviving sisters have dates and travel together to and from the dance. The sisters wear prim, old-fashioned dresses, but the modest clothing cannot conceal their beauty. At the prom they glow with exuberance as they joyfully experience life as normal teenage girls. Their drab world is suddenly filled with color as bright as the balloons that float down upon the dancers.

Lux and Trip are crowned prom queen and king and sneak off to the football field for a romantic encounter. Lux falls asleep and Trip runs off, leaving her to take a taxi home the next morning. Her furious parents respond to Lux's misbehavior by taking all the girls out of school and forcing them to stay in the house. The girls communicate with the boys in the neighborhood by signaling with flashlights. The boys answer by calling the girls on the phone and playing a song for them on the record player. The two groups of teens then swap songs over the phone line until they are forced to end the call.

Watching from the house across the street, the boys continue to spy on the girls. Intrigued, they see Lux meet with strange men on the roof of the Lisbon house after her parents are asleep. When the girls send a note to the boys to meet them late one night, the boys eagerly agree. They arrive to find Lux smoking in the doorway. She tells them to come in and wait for her sisters while she sits in the family's station wagon. The boys envision an exhilarating night of racing along the highway with a carload of girls. Instead, a brutal shock awaits them—Bonnie's dead body hanging in the basement. On their panicked escape from the house, they trip over the body of Therese, who has poisoned herself with pills. Paramedics load their bodies and that of Mary, who has gassed herself in the oven, into waiting ambulances. Lux, dead of carbon monoxide poisoning, joins her sisters at the morgue.

SOFIA COPPOLA

Sofia Coppola discusses the filming of *The Virgin Suicides* at the 2013 First Time Fest in New York City.

The movie ends as the narrator puzzles over the impossibility of understanding the events or forgetting them. As he speaks, the camera pans over the closed-up Lisbon house and the items left behind: a teapot, a lamp, a camera, a silver tiara. The score, a haunting instrumental piece, eerily echoes the emptiness of the scene.

The movie was shot on location in Toronto, Canada. Filming took twenty-nine days. Coppola cast several well-known actors in the film: Kathleen Turner as the girls' controlling mother; James Woods as the father; and Kirsten Dunst as Lux, whose rebellious streak results in the sisters' lockdown. Francis Coppola was one of the producers, and Sofia's brother Roman assisted with direction.

The film's premiere—at the Cannes Film Festival in France in May 1999—attracted praise for Coppola's debut movie. The movie won a spot in the festival's prestigious Directors Fortnight series.

Film critic Dustin Putman called *The Virgin Suicides* "a devastating, haunting motion picture of inconceivable power" after its screening at Cannes. By the film's American premiere—at the Sundance Film Festival in January 2000—many critics had joined in the praise for the movie, and for Coppola. "An assured and imaginative filmmaker," the *New York Times* called her. The film, the reviewer said, captured "both the triviality and the grandeur of youth." *The New Yorker* called Coppola's effort "a surprisingly intricate struggle with absence, grief, and memory." Her first feature, the critic wrote, showed Coppola to be "a master at rendering inner depths startlingly, straightforwardly visual." *The Virgin Suicides* earned Coppola an MTV Movie Award for best new filmmaker and the Young Hollywood award for best director. In May 2000, Paramount Classics agreed to handle distribution. The movie, with an estimated budget of $6 million, grossed more than $10.4 million worldwide at the box office.

The Virgin Suicides stars Kirsten Dunst, left, and A. J. Cook ham it up at the Sundance Film Festival in 2000.

3 SUCCESS STORY

While Sofia Coppola was putting the final touches on *The Virgin Suicides*, Spike Jonze was finishing his first feature film, *Being John Malkovich*. Like Coppola's film, Jonze's debut movie earned high marks from the critics. In June 1999, after both directors had completed their work on the films, they married. The wedding took place at the Francis Ford Coppola Vineyard in Napa Valley, California. Coppola wore a dress fashioned for her by designer John Galliano. Guests, including designer Marc Jacobs and Zoe Cassavetes, sipped on wine bottled in 1971, the year the bride was born. Francis Coppola made it a point to visit every table to describe each wine served. The celebrants toasted the couple with a brand of champagne named after Sofia. After the festivities, the newlyweds left for their honeymoon in Bora Bora, Tahiti. In its coverage of the wedding, *New York* magazine referred to Coppola as a "Hollywood hipster princess," and *Vogue* magazine called the couple "two of Hollywood's hottest young directors."

Sofia Coppola and
Spike Jonze in 2002.

After the hoopla of the wedding and the release of their debut films, the young directors took on new projects. Jonze directed several music videos and began work on his second film, *Adaptation*. Coppola appeared in a Marc Jacobs perfume ad and a music video for Phoenix's song, "Funky Squaredance," directed by her brother Roman. She and writer/director John Ridley created the TV series *Platinum*, the story of two brothers who build up a record company specializing in rap and hip hop. The show aired on the UPN network in 2003 but folded after a short run.

Lost and Found in Tokyo

Coppola also embarked on her second feature film, *Lost in Translation*. The tale of a disenchanted movie star and a bored and lonely young newlywed, *Lost in Translation* is a classic Sofia Coppola work. As she does in other films, Coppola relies on images rather than dialogue to portray her characters. "I don't want my movies to feel like movies," she said in an interview for *Directors Guild Association* magazine. "I want them to feel like life. People don't really express themselves that articulately in life." She points to the scene where the film's costar, Scarlett Johansson (as Charlotte), sits on the window ledge in her hotel room and gazes out at Tokyo. The young woman's loneliness and feelings of being lost come across loud and clear. "You project your feelings on her," Coppola said. "That's what I'm going for. I want the visual ways to tell the story rather than have the characters talk."

Coppola wrote and directed the film based on experiences from her own life, including her father's gig posing for a Suntory liquor ad filmed by Japanese director Akira Kurosawa in the mid-1970s. In her early twenties, Sofia visited Tokyo several times, where she worked on a friend's fashion show and found work as a photographer. She never considered filming the movie anywhere but Tokyo. "I love the way the neon at night looks [in Tokyo]," she said in an interview. The distant and unsatisfying relationship between Charlotte and her photographer husband John (played by Giovanni Ribisi) seemed to reflect Coppola's own troubled marriage. She and Jonze filed for divorce in December 2003.

The film begins with a shot of Charlotte, lying on her side on a bed. A voice welcomes visitors to Tokyo, and the camera zooms in on an obviously exhausted Bob Harris (Bill Murray) looking out a car window at the city's brilliant neon lights at night. He has come to Tokyo to film an ad for Suntory whisky. A movie actor whose fame has faded in the United States, Bob still has star power in Japan.

Charlotte has accompanied her husband to Tokyo, where he has an assignment as a fashion photographer. He leaves her on her own at the hotel while he travels to photo shoots. Bob spends his days filming the ad and trying to follow the instructions of a Japanese director whose sentences are reduced to a few words by the translator. Bob, confused, understands nothing of the Japanese words hurled at him. (Neither do moviegoers, unless they happen to speak Japanese.) The translator tells him: "He want you to turn, looking at camera. OK?" Bob, of course, knows something is lost in translation.

More is "lost in translation" than the director's words. Both Charlotte and Bob are in the midst of

Bill Murray and Scarlett Johansson share a few days in *Lost In Translation*.

crises in their lives. Charlotte, newly graduated from college, has no idea what she wants to do with her life. She is lonely in a marriage to a husband who doesn't understand her. Bob is lost in a mid-career slump and in a marriage that is "hard" but to which he is nevertheless committed. Charlotte and Bob are lost in Tokyo, confused by a culture and language not their own.

SOFIA COPPOLA

The two characters slowly become aware of each other at the hotel bar both frequent when they cannot sleep. They listen to one another, acknowledge each other's pain, and become intimate in the way friends—not lovers—do. In fact, there are no love scenes between them. The camera shows them exploring Tokyo as any American tourist might: visiting shrines, singing in a karaoke bar, and seeing the sights in the exotic city.

They know their time together is short. When they do part, Bob whispers into Charlotte's ear. The words are not audible, but it is clear that something meaningful has passed between them.

The film features several funny scenes. Bob worriedly asks if he has to dance with a TV talk show host billed as the "Japanese Johnny Carson," who insists on demonstrating a wacky dance routine during Bob's on-air interview. In another scene, Bob becomes trapped on an out-of-control treadmill in the hotel's exercise room.

Coppola insists that she wrote the script with Bill Murray in mind. Murray, however, proved difficult to track down. At one point she even called legendary actor Al Pacino to see if he would contact Murray for her. Eventually, the actor agreed to consider the role, but Coppola was not certain he would follow through until he showed up in Tokyo for the filming. Coppola was ecstatic. "I can't believe he's really coming to do a movie. It's my dream," she said when she heard he was on his way.

Challenges arose as soon as filming began in Tokyo in September 2002. Some members of the Japanese film crew did not speak English, and Coppola had to rely on the assistant director to communicate her wishes. A typhoon threatened Tokyo during the filming. The shots in public areas of

COPPOLA'S DIRECTING STYLE

On the set of *Marie Antoinette*, amid the opulent furnishings and lime green and magenta ball gowns, mile-high hairdos, and powdered wigs, Sofia Coppola projected a subdued image in her jeans and black T-shirt. Her screenwriting and directing are similarly subdued. Epic movies like the ones her father makes, such as *The Godfather* trilogy and *Apocalypse Now*, are not her style. Instead, she focuses on the interior story of her characters.

From her very first shots—usually taken with a handheld camera—Coppola brings the audience inside her character's head. The shots focus closely on a character who wistfully scans the world outside. "Sofia Coppola has captured the feeling of young people adrift in a seductive world," writes Carrie Rickey in *DGA Quarterly*. In other sequences, the camera looks over a person's shoulder, showing what the subject sees. "It's about getting close and closer to the character," Coppola explains.

She directs her cast with a light hand. "Having been in front of a camera, knowing

Sofia allowed Bill Murray to be himself in
Lost In Translation.

how vulnerable that can be, I am sensitive to
that vulnerability in my actors," Coppola told
Rickey. By all reports, Coppola is calm and quiet
on the set, a director who listens to actors
and may take their advice. When she decides to
do a scene her way, she gently guides the cast
in that direction. "She gets really good people
and lets them do their job," says G. Mac Brown,
producer of Coppola's film *Somewhere*.

Often Coppola allows actors to interpret
scenes for themselves. She sets the mood for them
and lets them take it from there. She basically
allowed Bill Murray to be himself in *Lost in
Translation*. Coppola's instructions to Murray
for the sushi bar scene were to "make (Scarlett
Johansson) laugh." He delivered a hilarious
improvisation. In the closing scene, it was
Murray's idea to whisper in Scarlett Johansson's
ear. Even Coppola did not know what he said.

the hotel where much of the movie was filmed could only be done after 1 a.m. to avoid disturbing the other guests. The city was noisy, with loudspeakers everywhere. The movie crew filmed in the subway, in the middle of the street, and from the second floor of the city's Starbucks, using available light whenever possible. One of the most challenging locations was at Shibuya Crossing in the heart of Tokyo's entertainment district. The intersection attracts huge crowds of pedestrians, especially young people. In one restaurant, the owner objected because the filming went over the allotted time. He pulled the plug on the lights, and kicked out the actors and crew. Coppola said that had never happened to her before.

Honors and Awards

Despite the challenges, Coppola's crew completed the filming in twenty-seven days, shooting six days a week. *Lost in Translation* premiered in the United States on August 29, 2003, at the Telluride Film Festival in Colorado. Its international premiere took place at the Venice Film Festival two days later. The screenings launched an avalanche of praise for Coppola's second movie.

Richard Corliss, *Time* magazine's top film critic, lauded *Lost in Translation* as a movie that "revels in contradictions. It's a comedy about melancholy, a romance without consummation, a travelogue that rarely hits the road." Peter Rainer of *New York* magazine called the film's contradictions "a heady, hallucinatory combo" and said Coppola had created "such empathy for Bob and Charlotte that our identification with them is almost total." Other critics noted Coppola's arrival as an accomplished

Sofia Coppola picked up an Oscar in 2004 for best original screenplay for *Lost In Translation.*

filmmaker. "With this film it becomes clear that Sofia Coppola is a filmmaker with eyes all her own," wrote critic David Ansen in *Newsweek*. "The beauty of *Lost in Translation* is in its exquisitely captured details." The *New York Times* called her "perhaps the most original and promising young female filmmaker in America."

The Academy of Motion Picture Arts and Sciences also took note of Coppola's excellence as a filmmaker by nominating her for its best director award in 2004. It was the first time in the academy's seventy-six-year history that an American woman had achieved that honor. At the time, only two other women directors had been nominated for the director's award—Italian filmmaker Lina Wertmüller for her 1976 film *Seven Beauties* and New Zealander Jane Campion for her film *The Piano* in 1993.

The film also earned Academy Award nominations for best picture, best original screenplay, and best actor. Coppola lost to Peter Jackson as best director. Jackson's big-budget *The Lord of the Rings: The Return of the King* collected that year's best picture award. The Oscar for best actor went to Sean Penn for his performance in *Mystic River*. However, Sofia Coppola did receive an Oscar for her screenplay, as well as the satisfaction of knowing that her artistic voice was being heard, and being hailed.

In accepting her screenwriting award, Coppola thanked the academy and those involved in producing the film, her brother Roman, her mother, her friends, her father "for everything he taught me," and her "muse," Bill Murray. Francis Coppola gave his daughter the thumbs-up and her mother and brother cheered as she walked to the stage.

The announcer noted that she represented the second family (the first was the Hustons) to have three generations of Oscar winners. In addition to Francis Ford Coppola's multiple wins, Sofia's grandfather, Carmine Coppola, had received an Oscar for the music score in his son's 1974 film *The Godfather: Part II*.

Lost in Translation collected many more awards. Among the most prestigious were Golden Globe awards for best motion picture, best actor (for Bill Murray), and best screenplay (for Coppola). When Murray received his Golden Globe award for his performance in the film, he commended Coppola for writing a script "so good" that every actor in the room was envious. Murray and Johansson both collected top awards from the British Academy of Film and Television Arts (BAFTA) for their performances in the film, and Sarah Flack received the BAFTA award for editing. The American Film Institute named *Lost in Translation* the movie of the year. The New York Film Critics gave top awards to Murray for his acting and Coppola for her directing.

Lost in Translation quickly achieved cult status. The Oscar nomination spurred even more attention from moviegoers. The film eventually showed in 882 U.S. theaters and played twenty-eight weeks. With an estimated budget of $4 million, *Lost in Translation* grossed almost $120 million worldwide.

4 RICH, FAMOUS, AND LONELY

Sofia Coppola turned to historical fiction for her third feature film, *Marie Antoinette*. Based on Antonia Fraser's novel *Marie Antoinette: The Journey*, the film showed a new side of the despised queen amid a spectacular cornucopia of lavish costumes and settings. In a video documenting the making of the movie—filmed by her mother, Eleanor—Coppola said her father told her to "throw a Marie Antoinette party and invite everyone to come to it in costume." She did just that, filling the screen with lush colors, rich fabrics, delectable foods, and impossibly elaborate hairdos.

Beyond the spectacle, however, Coppola explores an overlooked side of the teenage queen of France. The director's sympathetic portrayal of the future queen, played by Kirsten Dunst, shows Marie as a young, naive girl confined by tradition and court rules of behavior. Coppola's Marie is self-indulgent and bored, a "poor little rich girl" who is trapped in a sham marriage. "I wanted to make a personal story

Kirsten Dunst wore more than sixty gowns in Sofia Coppola's film *Marie Antoinette*.

and not a big epic historical biopic," Coppola told the *New York Times*.

The film is shot from the point of view of fourteen-year-old Marie, who has to leave her Austrian home and marry the fifteen-year-old boy who would become Louis XVI, played by Coppola's cousin Jason Schwartzman. Her marriage has been arranged by her mother to strengthen relations between Austria and France. Lonely and unhappy, she spends her time eating, getting her hair done, collecting new clothes, and partying with friends.

From the time she is delivered to Versailles aboard a horse-drawn coach, Marie Antoinette inhabits a luxurious make-believe world apart from the reality of poverty and unrest that swirls outside the palace gates. Though the French queen never said, "let them eat cake"—a myth that painted her as indifferent to the suffering of her people—the film's Marie ate plenty of cake herself. The food in the movie was so elaborate, in fact, that an entire department oversaw the production of pastries on display, and it brilliantly illustrated the decadence of the young queen's lifestyle. Coppola's Marie dresses in elaborate sherbet-colored gowns, acquires a closetful of shoes, and scandalizes the court by not following the strict rules of behavior expected of royalty.

When her husband's grandfather dies (his father had died earlier) and Marie Antoinette becomes queen, she continues her frivolous ways. Her subjects make the queen a target of their hatred, as food shortages and poverty lead to riots and unrest.

After eight years of marriage, Marie Antoinette gives birth to a long-awaited child, a daughter. Toning down her social life, she spends time with her family, enjoying nature and the garden at her cottage on the grounds of Versailles. The palace cannot insulate the royals from the real world forever, however. As the movie ends, the royal family is swept up in the turmoil of the French Revolution. Forced to leave the palace, they board a coach and head out to meet their destiny. The film ends before the king and queen lose their heads to the guillotine.

Marie Antoinette, Coppola said, was the third in a trilogy of films about young women who are going through painful and lonely transitions in their lives. "It's a continuation of the other films—sort of about a lonely girl in a big hotel or palace or whatever, kind of wandering around, trying to grow up... This is a story about a girl becoming a woman." To illustrate this, Coppola presents Marie Antoinette's life as a personal story told from the fresh eye of youth. The pop music she used for the soundtrack lends an energy to the scenes and transforms Marie Antoinette into someone who is relevant to today's audiences.

Filming took place on location in France at one of the country's most magnificent architectural treasures—the Château de Versailles, the sprawling palace where Marie Antoinette and the royal family actually lived in the late 1700s. Now a national monument, the palace houses the Museum of the History of France. The overseer of the elegant château welcomed Coppola's crew, allowing them access to areas of the palace not usually open to tourists. Coppola told the *New York Times* that the head of the palace told them, "This is your home." During twelve weeks of filming in the spring of 2005, the crew captured shots of Marie Antoinette's private theater and the palace's immense Hall of Mirrors. To recreate the château of the 1700s, the film's decorators completely refurnished the rooms. Museum officials supported the film because it put a

Marie Antoinette went to this small chateau—called the Petit Trianon, on the grounds of the Palace of Versailles—to escape the French court and enjoy the gardens that surrounded the estate.

spotlight on France and its rich history. The director of Versailles "liked that I was attempting to tell the story from [Marie's] point of view and really opened Versailles to us," Coppola said.

The movie's opening sparked a frenzy of interest in the real Marie Antoinette. Merchants sold goods with a Marie Antoinette theme, magazines gave the queen cover billing, and books and talk shows focused on her to capitalize on the fad.

SOFIA COPPOLA

Raves and Rants

Coppola won the Cinema Prize of the French National Education System at the Cannes Film Festival and was nominated for the Palme d'Or award, the festival's top honor, given to the director of the best feature film (it went to Ken Loach for *The Wind That Shakes the Barley*). Only one woman director, Jane Campion, has won the award since its introduction in 1955.

Marie Antoinette elicited raves and rants from both critics and moviegoers. When the movie premiered at Cannes in May 2006, the audience responded with applause and boos. Some French viewers might have disapproved of Coppola's handling of the Revolution's most hated icon. Nevertheless, more than one million film fans viewed the movie in France between its release there in May and the U.S. premiere at the New York Film Festival in October.

U.S. critics exhibited similar contradictory responses. The *New York Times* posted reviews that expressed both views. *Times* reporter A. O. Scott noted the parallels between the film's eighteenth century over-the-top decadence and that of modern Hollywood. Coppola used her intimate knowledge of that world to create a character "so personal, so genuine, so knowing," the *Times* reviewer wrote. "I for one am happy to lose my head over *Marie Antoinette*."

Scott's counterpart, Manohla Dargis, insisted that Coppola "ignores what's best about Marie Antoinette's story" — her role in turning the French people against the monarchy. "It soon becomes clear," Dargis wrote, "that the director is herself bewitched by these [court] rituals, which she repeats again and again."

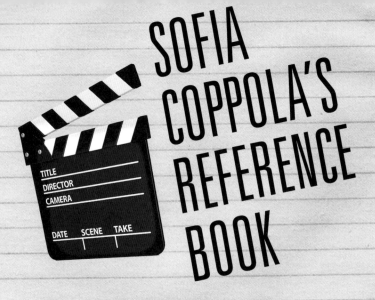

SOFIA COPPOLA'S REFERENCE BOOK

Sofia Coppola envisions the scenes in her movies long before the camera starts to roll. She does not write out every word of dialogue. Instead, she aims for a mood and a sense of the characters. She collects images, photographs, and drawings that illustrate the mood she is trying to capture in a little yellow book, which she frequently consults on the set. Richard Beggs, the sound designer for Coppola's film *Somewhere*, notes that Coppola "thinks in terms of images."

Her reference book of images helps the production designer set the scene and the cinematographer get exactly the shot Coppola wants. "Sofia and I always work from the details out, and she is very specific on those," says Anne Ross, production designer for *Somewhere*. "Sofia knows what she wants; she will calmly give a concise opinion about why she likes or doesn't like something."

G. Mac Brown was the producer for Sofia Coppola's film *Somewhere*.

The idea behind the opening scene in *Lost in Translation*—the shot of Scarlett Johansson lying on her side—came from a John Kacere painting. Coppola included a photo of the painting in her reference book, as well as snapshots of Tokyo sights, views from the Park Hyatt Tokyo hotel, and a photo of the hotel bar singer—a regular on the Tokyo circuit who would later play that role in the film.

"One of the best and worst things about Sofia is that she knows exactly what she wants, which makes it really easy" to work with her, says G. Mac Brown, producer of *Somewhere*. "But that's the only thing she wants, which makes it really hard."

Other critics either liked the film or hated it. *Rolling Stone* lauded Coppola's efforts: "With lyrical intelligence and scrappy wit, Coppola creates a luscious world to get lost in. It's a pleasure." *Toronto Star* critic Susan Walker took an opposite view, saying Coppola squandered a "once-in-a-lifetime opportunity to film [at] the Palace of Versailles," to show only "the trappings … at the expense of any substance." The film's lack of attention to historical events triggered other negative comments about Coppola's production. But those criticisms, according to film critic Ebert, "would alter [the film's] fragile magic and reduce its romantic and tragic poignancy to the level of an instructional film." The movie, he said, never intended to be informative about the political events of eighteenth century France.

It was no surprise when the movie won an Oscar for best costume design at the 2007 Academy Awards. Kirsten Dunst wore more than sixty gowns during her portrayal of Marie Antoinette, all of which were designed by Milena Canonero. It was, however, the movie's only nomination.

A $40 million production, the movie was a massive undertaking. "After *Marie Antoinette*, I was over movies," the director told the *Hollywood Reporter*. The film grossed almost $16 million in the United States and nearly $45 million worldwide.

While in France for the filming of *Marie Antoinette*, Coppola renewed her acquaintance with Thomas Mars, who had worked on the soundtrack of *The Virgin Suicides*. The friendship deepened into love. In November 2006 the couple's first child, a daughter they named Romy, was born. Coppola took the next few years off to rest and spend time with her daughter. Romy's sister, Cosima, joined the family three and a half years later.

Sofia Coppola and her future husband, Thomas Mars, arrive at a party in Paris in 2005.

The couple married on August 29, 2011, in the town of Bernalda in southern Italy, the birthplace of Coppola's great-grandfather. The ceremony took place in the garden of a *palazzo* owned by Sofia's family. Film director George Lucas joined a small gathering of friends and family for the simple wedding, performed by Bernalda's mayor in a civil ceremony. The bride's father walked her down the aisle.

5 SOMEWHERE AND BEYOND

By 2009, Sofia Coppola was ready to tackle another movie. After the huge effort required to produce *Marie Antoinette*, the director wanted to focus on a simpler project for her fourth feature film. She said her goal was to create "a mood, more like a poem, a portrait of [a] person."

The person Coppola created in her screenplay for *Somewhere*—Johnny Marco, played by Stephen Dorff—is a bored bad-boy actor whose life revolves around drink, pills, women, his Ferrari, and sleep. His self-absorbed existence is disrupted when his eleven-year-old daughter, Cleo, played by Elle Fanning, comes to stay with him at the hotel where he lives.

"I had just had my first daughter, so I was thinking about how that changes your perspective and your priorities," Coppola said before the U.S. premiere of *Somewhere*.

Filming took place in June and July 2009 with a relatively small budget of between $7 million and

Sofia Coppola based some moments in her film *Somewhere* on her childhood experiences.

Stephen Dorff said Johnny Marco in
Somewhere was his most challenging role.

$8 million. Shooting required about eight weeks
and took place in California and Italy. Like *Lost in
Translation*, Coppola's fourth feature film takes place
in a hotel, this time the Chateau Marmont in West
Hollywood. The hotel itself becomes a character in
the film with its reputation as a retreat for celebrities,
its old-world aura, and its long-serving staff. Coppola
had stayed at the hotel several times as a child
during trips with her family. She knew longtime staff
members like Romulo Laki, the "singing waiter"
who serenaded diners accompanied by his guitar.
In *Somewhere* he plays a sweet rendition of "Teddy
Bear" to Cleo, the song he had strummed for a
young Coppola during one of her childhood visits.
    Much of the movie takes place within the hotel,
in apartment-like suites that contain their own

full-sized kitchens. The hotel's owner, André Balazs, allowed Coppola to film there because he "had an inherent trust of her deep knowledge of what makes the Chateau so special and [knew] that it would be brought to her movie," according to Philip Pavel, general manager of the Chateau. Pavel said he was eager to have people view the movie and see "the Chateau's sweet side. I believe it's what makes the place so special; there is a homey feeling, and a feeling of safety."

During filming, Dorff lived at the Chateau, mimicking the life of his character. "By living there," Dorff said in an article, "I experienced a lot of what Johnny would have." Dorff even ordered his own Chateau stationery, imprinted with Johnny Marco's name. "On this movie," he said, "I tried to live the part more." Dorff called his portrayal of Johnny Marco "the most challenging role of my career by far." It was a role, he said, that his mother, who had died the previous year, would have wanted him to play.

Little Dialogue

The film opens with shots of Marco's Ferrari as it speeds around a racetrack. The monotonous loop continues for almost five minutes. Another ten minutes pass before anyone speaks a word. There is little dialogue throughout the movie. Instead, Coppola relies on the actors' visual responses to each situation and to the other characters. The script for the entire movie was about forty-eight pages, only half the usual length for a film. In many scenes, Dorff and Fanning had only a few lines of dialogue; the rest of the time the actors improvised. "I [made] up histories in my head and remember[ed] stories

SOFIA SLEPT HERE

Sofia Coppola's connections and experiences as the daughter of Francis Ford Coppola helped her gain entrance into an exclusive world. In one scene in *Somewhere*, Cleo and Johnny swim in a private spa in the presidential suite of the luxurious Principe di Savoia, described by the film's producer, G. Mac Brown, as "the nicest hotel suite in the world."

At first the manager of the Principe di Savoia refused to talk with the filmmakers about shooting in the presidential suite, which is reserved for the likes of Madonna, Saudi princesses, and international celebrities. Coppola, however, had stayed in the hotel's presidential suite with her family. That history, along with her persuasive skills, opened the doors.

to have in mind," Dorff said. In one scene, Marco sits inert and silent as he waits—along with the audience—for several long minutes while a mask of plaster dries on his head.

At the Chateau, Marco follows a numbingly empty routine. Then Cleo arrives on the scene. Her presence forces him to go outside his hideaway to the world beyond. He watches as his daughter twirls around an ice rink. They play Guitar Hero together. She cooks for him and travels with him to Italy, where Johnny receives a film award.

As the movie progresses, Marco becomes attached to his daughter and begins to reassess his own life. When Cleo leaves for summer camp (via an impromptu helicopter ride), Marco feels the loss. As the movie ends, Marco checks out of the Chateau Marmont, drives his Ferrari into the middle of nowhere, parks on the side of the road, leaves the keys in the ignition, and silently walks away, a half smile slowly forming on his face. The ending is reminiscent of the Ferrari's opening scene as the car zooms around an empty track. This time, presumably, Marco leaves the emptiness behind.

Coppola used much material from her own life for *Somewhere*. As a young girl, she took a helicopter ride with her famous father, accompanied him to film award ceremonies and other adults-only venues, lived in hotels, and put up with the entourage that accompanies a celebrity and his family. "I feel like everyone should tell what they know in the world that they know," she said during a *New York Times* interview. She also told reporters that *Somewhere* was not autobiographical. She had experienced Johnny Marco's world, but her father was not the character in the movie, and her childhood was not Cleo's.

Sofia Coppola accepts the Golden Lion award from director Quentin Tarantino at the Venice Film Festival in 2010.

Another Milestone

The movie made a huge splash at its premiere at the Venice International Film Festival in September 2010. The judges awarded Coppola the festival's top prize, the Golden Lion award, for *Somewhere*. She became one of only five Americans and one of only four women to win the honor, which goes to the year's best film internationally. Film director Quentin Tarantino, president of the festival's jury, said the film "enchanted us from the first and it grew and grew in our hearts, in our analysis, in our minds and affections."

In accepting the award, Coppola thanked the festival for the "tremendous honor" and said she believed it would help *Somewhere* "reach more of an audience." She also thanked her father for "teaching me" about films.

Tarantino, who had dated Coppola after her split with Spike Jonze, said at the press conference after the presentation that he had not swayed the voting in any way and that the selection of *Somewhere* was unanimous. Coppola said she hoped her movie's award would encourage others to make "small personal films."

Somewhere premiered in the United States on December 22, 2010. Soon after, the National Board of Review honored Coppola with a special achievement award for writing, directing, and producing the film and placed it on its list of the top ten independent movies of the year. Once again Coppola received mixed responses to her work. She collected both awed praise and harsh rejections. The *New York Times* called the movie "exquisite, melancholy and formally audacious." Coppola had created "something marvelous" with the "power to refresh your perceptions and deepen your sympathies," the *Times* critic wrote in his review of *Somewhere*. He likened watching the film to reading a poem, with scenes that "play off one another like stanzas." What emerges from the director's "careful, watchful, slow" shots, he wrote, is "a sad and affecting story … about a father's loneliness and a daughter's devotion."

Like the *Times* reviewer, the majority of critics gave the movie high marks. Some, however, blasted the film. Its slow pace—which Coppola said gave viewers a chance to experience the characters' feelings—irritated more than a few viewers. "There are multiple scenes where she doesn't realize that the shot is going on for far too long," wrote the *Examiner*'s critic. The movie, he said, "lacked substance" and was filled with slower moments that "don't really add up to much of anything."

Movie Nation's reviewer called the film "a triumph of tedium, banality passing for depth, a vacuous embrace of nothing."

The movie did not have wide appeal among American audiences. At its peak, the film was shown at eighty-three U.S. movie houses. It grossed less than $2 million in the United States. Worldwide sales neared $14 million.

Celebrity Shopping Spree

Coppola's fifth feature film, *The Bling Ring*, takes a hard look at America's obsession with celebrity and material goods. It is based on the true story of a group of Southern California teenagers who stole jewelry and designer clothes worth at least $3 million from the homes of Hollywood stars. They found their way to the homes of Lindsay Lohan, Paris Hilton, and others on the star circuit by researching the celebrities' addresses on Google. At some of the stops, the teen gang merely walked in the door and helped themselves to the expensive clothes and jewels they saw. Their illegal "shopping spree," in 2008 and 2009, lasted nine months. The gang, dubbed the "bling ring," robbed Hilton's home six times before the star noticed anything was missing.

Coppola first became interested in the story when she read about the real teens' exploits in a *Vanity Fair* article. Believing that the story would make a good movie, she researched the rights and discovered no other director had made an offer. She negotiated a deal and began writing the script. It was the first time she had written a script based on an actual crime story. The crew began filming the movie in March 2012.

Sofia Coppola attends the 2013 premiere of her film *The Bling Ring* with cast members, from left, Claire Julien, Emma Watson of *Harry Potter* fame, and Taissa Farga.

The movie opens with a group of hooded teens sneaking through the dark into a luxurious house. "Let's go shopping!" one girl says. And they do, reaching into drawers, jewelry boxes, and closets to make their selections from a huge collection of shoes, jewels, purses, makeup, and clothes. Green surveillance tape shows the gang leaving the premises. In daylight, the camera pans the wealthy neighborhood of Calabasas, California, then focuses on Nicki (a convicted member of the "bling ring" played by Emma Watson), who announces to members of the media that the episode has been a "huge learning experience" that may someday lead to her being head of a country.

A year earlier, Marc Hall, played by Israel Broussard, initially the sole male member of the Bling Ring, is the new kid at a Los Angeles County

UNLIMITED ACCESS

Sofia Coppola's celebrity helped convince Paris Hilton (left) to allow her inside Hilton's Malibu mansion for two weeks of filming. "The only reason I agreed to do it at all is because it's Sofia," Hilton told reporter Kyle Buchanan. "I have so much respect for her and I think she's an incredibly talented director. And the movie is amazing."

The movie shows Hilton's house as the teens break in, excitedly paw through her clothes and jewelry, and take what they want. The scenes brought tears to Hilton's eyes when she viewed them at a party after the movie's premiere at the Cannes Film Festival in May 2013. "I was like, 'Oh my God, this really happened to me,'" Hilton said. "It's so violating. It just made me really angry and upset, and when I see these kids, I want to, like, slap them."

school for dropouts. Celebrity-crazed Rebecca Ahn, played by Katie Chang, befriends him and soon lures him into a shoplifting excursion. The two join friends at a nightclub, where they spot heiress Hilton, Kirsten Dunst, and other stars. When Marc later discovers that Hilton will be out of town, the teens decide to break into her palatial house. They steal her clothes and jewelry, and flaunt their loot to gain status and attention. Soon their friends are accompanying them on their night visits to celebrities' homes.

The teens repeat their burglaries at the homes of other celebrities, including TV personality Audrina Patridge, actress Megan Fox, and English actor Orlando Bloom. They sell the goods to a shady dealer who is dating one of the girls. The release of grainy security tape showing them burglarizing Patridge's house fails to deter them. In fact, they brag about their exploits on Facebook. The tapes and their online postings eventually lead to their arrests.

Eventually, Marc admits everything to police, Rebecca offers to trade information for a break on the charges against her, and Nicki blames her troubles on everyone else and later uses her notoriety to direct teens to her website. She shares a cellblock with Lindsay Lohan, one of the victims of the teens' burglaries.

The film shows the events from the point of view of the teen thieves. The use of "selfies," photos shot by the subject, reinforces that viewpoint. Coppola said she wanted to allow the movie audience "to experience it through [the teens'] eyes."

Coppola said the story "summed up everything that I think is declining in our culture." The teens saw what society valued, and did whatever it took to get those things for themselves. As a parent, she fears

Sofia Coppola and her daughter Cosima in Italy in 2011. The film director has expressed concern over the effect of America's celebrity-crazed culture on her children's generation.

the effects of a culture that glorifies celebrity. She said in a *New York Times* magazine interview that her daughter's six-year-old friends were already saying they want to be famous, a trend that unnerves Coppola.

The Bling Ring opened strong in limited U.S. theaters on June 14, 2013, and expanded nationwide the following weekend. With an estimated $15 million budget, the film grossed $5.8 million in the U.S. market and about $19 million worldwide.

Critic Richard Roeper gave the film an "A-" and called Emma Watson's portrayal of Nicki "comedic gold." Another reviewer said the film achieved "what Coppola does better than almost anybody else: peeling back layers of excess to find single, simple truths. It challenges audiences to engage with and confront a society we've allowed to happen through unhealthy obsessions with reality television and hero worship."

Despite generally positive reviews, the movie received little mention at awards time. However, Coppola won the 2013 Dorothy Arzner Directors Award from the Women in Film organization.

Following Her Passion

Coppola acknowledged that the movie business is "dominated by men" and that "every now and then" she has encountered roadblocks because she is a woman. The business has changed in recent years, she said, with more studio executives and film directors who are women, "so there will be more female points of view." Coppola produces her own films, so she has not been too frustrated by Hollywood's resistance to women's projects. "I've been able to do what I want to do," she said.

Rather than selecting movie topics that will appeal to major studios, Coppola chooses projects that interest her. "You have to find something you are really excited and passionate about because you spend such a long time working on it," she said. "It has to stay in your interest for three years—to make it and promote it—so it has to have enough to make you want to put that effort in."

Coppola's next project is a film based on the acclaimed *Fairyland: A Memoir of My Father* by Alysia Abbott.

"I love the book *Fairyland*," Coppola said in a press release. "It's a sweet and unique love story of a girl and her dad, both growing up in 1970s San Francisco."

It sounds just like a Sofia Coppola film.

FILMOGRAPHY

The following is a list of the films, shorts, videos, and television projects Sofia Coppola has either directed, written, produced, served as executive producer for, or acted in as of this writing. The titles are listed in alphabetical order by year. For a more complete listing, please visit the Internet Movie Database website, www.IMDb.com

The Godfather (1972 / uncredited) (actress)

The Godfather: Part II (1974 / uncredited) (actress)

Rumble Fish (1983 / as Domino Coppola) (actress)

The Cotton Club (1984 / as Domino Coppola) (actress)

Frankenweenie (1984 / as Domino Coppola) (actress)

The Princess Who Had Never Laughed (1984 / as Domino Coppola) (actress)

Faerie Tale Theatre: The Princess Who Had Never Laughed (1986 / as Domino Coppola) (actress)

Peggy Sue Got Married (1986 / actress)

Anna (1987 / actress)

New York Stories—"Life Without Zoe" (1989 / writer)

The Godfather: Part III (1990 / actress)

The Spirit of '76 (1990 / uncredited) (actress)

Inside Monkey Zetterland (1992 / actress)

Ciao L.A. (1994 / actress, producer)

Hi Octane (1994 / producer, executive producer)

Bed, Bath and Beyond (1996 / director)

Lick the Star (short) (1998 / director, writer, producer)

Star Wars: Episode I—The Phantom Menace (1999 / actress)

The Virgin Suicides (1999 / director, writer)

Beastie Boys: Video Anthology (2000 / producer)

CQ (2001 / actress)

Lost in Translation (2003 / director, writer, producer)

Platinum (2003 / executive producer, writer)

VOID (Video Overview in Deceleration) (segment "This Here Giraffe") (2005 / director)

Marie Antoinette (2006 / director, writer, producer)

Somewhere (2010 / director, writer, producer)

Between Two Ferns with Zach Galifianakis (2013 / uncredited) (actress)

The Bling Ring (2013 / director, writer, producer)

GLOSSARY

Academy Award—Award of excellence given to a film and/or its cast and crew by the Academy of Motion Picture Arts and Sciences. Also commonly called an "Oscar."

box office—The place where movie tickets are sold; income from ticket sales.

cameo—A brief appearance in a film, often not mentioned in the credits.

cinematographer—Professional in charge of photography used in making a movie; cameraman.

cult status—A person or thing favored by certain groups of people over an extended period

director—The person who oversees the shooting, the acting and other aspects of a movie.

Golden Globe®—Top honor for the year's best in film and TV awarded by the Hollywood Foreign Press Association.

Golden Lion—Top prize awarded by the Venice International Film Festival for the best film of the year.

Golden Raspberry (Razzie) Award—Prize given by the Golden Raspberry Awards Foundation for the worst film performances of the year; a tongue-in-cheek award.

grossed—Earned; the gross is the total amount of money a movie earns, not including expenses.

icon—A person who is seen as a symbol of something.

internship—On-the-job training to learn a craft, usually for little or no pay.

lead—The starring role in a movie or play.

movie score—Music accompanying a film.

movie set—The studio or area where a movie is performed and filmed.

on location—The area where a movie is filmed, usually the real setting of a movie or a place that resembles the actual locale.

Palme d'Or—The top award of the Cannes Film Festival, presented to the year's best movie.

point of view—Position or angle from which something is viewed; in movies, the technique of shooting a scene from the viewpoint of a character or of the director or writer.

premiere—The first showing of a film.

producer—The person in charge of providing, or arranging for, the money to make a movie.

screenplay—A written form of a movie that includes detailed directions for lighting, movements, and other aspects involved in the filming process.

stage name—Name used by an actor instead of his or her real name.

Valley Girl—Young woman from Southern California who talks using a particular accent or slang.

BIBLIOGRAPHY

Cook, Pam, and Yvonne Tasker, ed. *Fifty Contemporary Film Directors*. Oxford and New York: Routledge, 2010.

Coppola, Eleanor, director. "The Making of *Marie Antoinette*." *Marie Antoinette* DVD. Sony Pictures, 2007.

Cowie, Peter, *Coppola: A Biography*. Cambridge, MA: Da Capo Press, 1994.

Dargis, Manohla, and A. O. Scott. "'Marie Antoinette': Best or Worst of Times?" *New York Times*, May 25, 2006.

Fuller, Graham. "Sofia Coppola's Second Chance." *New York Times*, April 16, 2000.

Galloway, Stephen. "Sofia Coppola: The Trials, Tears and Talent." *The Hollywood Reporter*, May 8, 2013.

Gerosa, Melina. "Goddaughter." *Entertainment Weekly*, January 25, 1991.

Hirschbert, Lynn. "The Coppola Smart Mob." *New York Times Magazine*, August 31, 2003.

Lim, Dennis. "It's What She Knows: The Luxe Life." *New York Times*, December 10, 2010.

"Lost in Location—Lost in Translation Behind the Scenes." YouTube, posted July 21, 2012. http://www.youtube.com/watch?v=EAp50ZLMqXc

MUSEproductions. "2000 Sundance Film Festival, *Virgin Suicides* Q & A." YouTube, posted April 21, 2008. http://www.youtube.com/watch?v=dBo1XSo5mW0

Radziwill, Lee. "In Conversation: Lee Radziwill and Sofia Coppola, on Protecting Privacy." *New York Times T Magazine*, May 30, 2013.

Scott, A. O. "The Pampered Life, Viewed From the Inside," *New York Times*, December 21, 2010.

"Sofia Coppola: Sadness & Splendor." *The Hollywood Reporter*, May 9, 2013.

SOURCE NOTES

Chapter 1

Pg. 11: Radziwill, Lee, "In Conversation: Lee Radziwill and Sofia Coppola, on Protecting Privacy," *New York Times T magazine*, May 30, 2013.

Pg. 14: Scott, A. O., "The Pampered Life, Viewed From the Inside," *New York Times*, December 21, 2010.

Pg. 17: Fuller, Graham, "Sofia Coppola's Second Chance," *New York Times*, April 16, 2000.

Chapter 2

Pg. 18: Rickey, Carrie, "Lost and Found," *DGA Quarterly*, Spring 2013.

Pg. 22: Cook, Pam, and Yvonne Tasker, ed. "Sofia Coppola," in *Fifty Contemporary Film Directors*, p. 128.

Pg. 23: "2000 Sundance Film Festival, *Virgin Suicides* Q & A, http://www.youtube.com/watch?v=dBo1XSo5mW0

Chapter 3

Pg. 35: Murray, Rebecca, "Behing-the-Scenes of 'Lost in Translation' with Sofia Coppola," About.com Hollywood Movies.

Pg. 40: Corliss, Richard, "A Victory for Lonely Hearts," *Time* magazine, September 15, 2003.

Pg. 40: Rainer, Peter, "Sleepless in Tokyo," *New York* magazine, September 15, 2003.

Chapter 4

Pgs. 44, 46: Hohenadel, Kristin, "French Royalty as Seen by Hollywood Royalty," *New York Times*, September 10, 2006.

Chapter 5

Pg. 59: Lim, Dennis, "It's What She Knows: The Luxe Life," *New York Times*, December 10, 2010.

Pg. 64: Buchanan, Kyle, "Cannes: Paris Hilton Cried While Watching *The Bling Ring*," Vulture.com, May 17, 2013.

Pg. 65: Vishnevetsky, Ignatly, "Bling Ring," *Chicago Sun-Times*, June 21, 2013.

FURTHER INFORMATION

Books

Caldwell, Thomas. *The Film Analysis Handbook*. Cheltenham, Australia: Insight Publications, 2011.

Delorme, Stéphane. *Masters of Cinema: Francis Ford Coppola*. London, England: Phaidon Press, 2010.

Espejo, Roman. *Celebrity Culture* (Opposing Viewpoints). Farmington Hills, MI: Greenhaven Press, 2010.

Kooperman, Paul. *Screenwriting: Script to Screen*. Cheltenham, Australia: Insight Publications, 2011.

Krossing, Karen. *Cut the Lights*. Custer, WA: Orca Book Publishers, 2013.

Lanier, Troy, and Clay Nichols. *Filmmaking for Teens: Pulling Off Your Shorts*. Studio City, CA: Wiese, Michael Productions, 2010.

Mayle, Simon. *How Harry Riddles Made a Mega-amazing Zombie Movie* (Shoutykid). New York, NY: HarperCollins Children's Books, 2014.

Meyer, Carolyn. *The Bad Queen: Rules and Instructions for Marie-Antoinette* (Young Royals). Boston, MA: HMH Books for Young Readers, 2011.

O'Connor, Mimi. *Reel Culture*. San Francisco, CA: Zest Books, 2009.

O'Neill, Joseph. *Movie Director* (21st Century Skills Library: Cool Careers). North Mankato, MN: Cherry Lake Publishing, 2013.

Phaidon Press, eds. *Take 100: The Future of Film: 100 New Directors*. London, England: Phaidon Press, 2010.

Rausch, Andrew J. *Obsessed With Hollywood: Test Your Knowledge of the Silver Screen*. San Francisco, CA: Chronicle Books, 2007.

Williams, Dar. *Lights, Camera, Amalee*. Grand Haven, MI: Brilliance Audio, 2011.

Yager, Fred, Jan Yager, and David Carradine. *Career Opportunities in the Film Industry*. Checkmark Books, 2009.

On the Web
www.boxoffice.com
www.boxofficemojo.com
These websites contain financial data such as box-office grosses and other information on movies including showtime and release schedules.

www.imdb.com
The Internet Movie Database contains a plethora of information on movie trends, directors, celebrity news, and film trailers.

www.pinterest.com/removealldoubt/ style-icon-sofia-coppola/
The Pinterest website has a large collection of photos illustrating the fashion and style of Sofia Coppola.

INDEX

Page numbers in **boldface** are illustrations.

ABOUT THE AUTHOR

Susan Dudley Gold is a writer, historian, and movie buff. She has written several books that feature women and their roles in current events, including *Roberts v. U.S. Jaycees: Women's Rights*. She is the author of two books in Cavendish Square's Great Filmmakers series—*Kathyrn Bigelow* and *Sofia Coppola*—and five books in the publisher's First Amendment Cases series.

In the 1980s, Gold produced, directed, and wrote a thirty-minute video, "The 10th Year: Maine's Fishing Industry, 1976–1985," which was screened at the statewide Maine Fishermen's Forum.

Gold worked as a newspaper reporter and magazine editor before becoming a graphic designer and children's book author. She has written more than fifty books for middle- and high-school students on a wide range of topics. She has received numerous honors for her writing and design work, including a Carter G. Woodson Honor Book award for *United States v. Amistad: Slave Ship Mutiny* (Supreme Court Milestones), and a Junior Library Guild Selection for *Son of Sam Case* in the First Amendment Cases series.

Gold and her husband own a web design and publishing business in Maine. They have one son and two grandchildren.